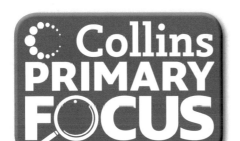

Vocabulary

Pupil Book 2

Louis Fidge and Sarah Lindsay

William Collins' dream of knowledge for all began with the publication of his first book in 1819. A self-educated mill worker, he not only enriched millions of lives, but also founded a flourishing publishing house. Today, staying true to this spirit, Collins books are packed with inspiration, innovation and practical expertise. They place you at the centre of a world of possibility and give you exactly what you need to explore it.

Collins. Freedom to teach.

Published by Collins
An imprint of HarperCollins*Publishers* Ltd.
77–85 Fulham Palace Road
Hammersmith
London
W6 8JB

**Browse the complete Collins catalogue at
www.collinseducation.com**

Text © Louis Fidge and Sarah Lindsay 2013
Design and illustrations © HarperCollins*Publishers* Limited 2013

Previously published as *Collins Primary Writing*, first published 1998; and *Collins Focus on Writing*, first published 2002.

10 9 8 7 6 5 4 3 2 1

ISBN: 978-0-00-750101-4

Louis Fidge and Sarah Lindsay assert their moral right to be identified as the authors of this work.

British Library Cataloguing in Publication Data
A Catalogue record for this publication is available from the British Library.

Cover template: Laing & Carroll
Cover illustration: Paul McCaffrey
Series design: Neil Adams
Illustrations: Stephanie Dix and James Walmesley.
Some illustrations have been reused from the previous edition (978-0-00-713227-1).

Printed and bound by Printing Express Limited, Hong Kong.

MIX
Paper from
responsible sources
FSC™ C007454

FSC™ is a non-profit international organisation established to promote the responsible management of the world's forests. Products carrying the FSC label are independently certified to assure consumers that they come from forests that are managed to meet the social, economic and ecological needs of present and future generations, and other controlled sources.

Find out more about HarperCollins and the environment at
www.harpercollins.co.uk/green

Contents

Definitions

A **definition** is the **meaning** of a word.

Dinosaurs were huge animals that roamed the Earth a long time ago.

This is how Gurdip defines dinosaurs.

Dinosaurs were large reptiles that lived in prehistoric times.

This is a **dictionary definition** of dinosaurs.

Dinosaurs – large prehistoric reptiles.

This is an even shorter way of defining dinosaurs.

Practice

These words and definitions have got mixed up. Copy the words and write the correct definition for each word. Use a dictionary to help you.

1. centipede   a house built on one level only

2. yak   the woolly coat from a sheep

3. bungalow   a small crawling insect with many legs

4. monastery   a large number of musicians who play music together

5. quiver   a long-haired ox from the Himalayas

6. architect   a case for holding arrows

7. fleece   someone who plans and designs new buildings

8. orchestra   a place where monks live and work

More to think about

Write your own definitions for the following words.

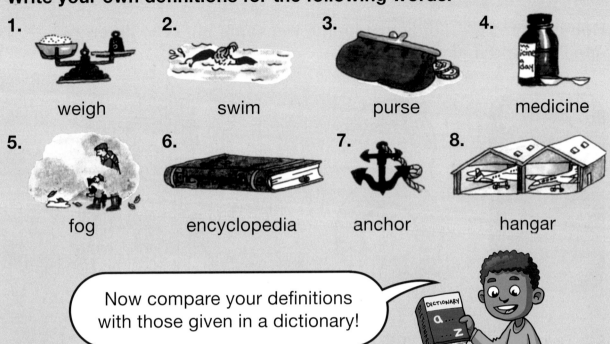

1. weigh
2. swim
3. purse
4. medicine
5. fog
6. encyclopedia
7. anchor
8. hangar

Now compare your definitions with those given in a dictionary!

Now try these

Re-write these dictionary definitions.
Use as few words as possible.

1. panda   The giant panda is a rare, black and white, bear-like animal that lives in the bamboo forests of China.

2. aviary   An aviary is a large outdoor cage for keeping birds.

3. vaccinate   When a doctor vaccinates you, he or she injects you with a substance to protect you from disease.

4. aspirin   This is a drug made into a tablet that is used to treat headaches and minor pains.

5. desert   A desert is a dry wasteland where few things grow.

6. dessert   A dessert is a sweet or a pudding eaten after the main course.

Homophones

Homophones are words that **sound the same** but have **different spellings and meanings**.

eight   ate

Say the words **eight** and **ate** aloud.
They sound the same.
They are **spelled differently** and have **different meanings**.

Practice

Write the correct homophone to match the picture.
Use a dictionary to help you.

1.

   dough or **doe**

2.

   fir or **fur**

3.

   write or **right**

4.

   ruff or **rough**

5.

   stair or **stare**

6.

   son or **sun**

More to think about

1. Copy the sentence. Choose the correct homophone.

   a) Rakesh wasn't sure (weather/whether) to have another sweet.

   b) "I can't (hear/here) you," shouted the man.

   c) Emma and Lee couldn't (weight/wait) until Christmas.

   d) Stuart (through/threw) the ball so hard it went over the school fence!

   e) The bus (fare/fair) was £2.50.

   f) "(Witch/Which) picture is mine?" asked Kathy.

2. Copy the homophones you haven't used in Question 1. Write a sentence using each one.

Now try these

1. Write your own definition for each of the words in the boxes. Use your dictionary to help if you need to.

saw sore soar		rain reign rein
road rowed rode		vein vane vain

2. Write a sentence that has **to**, **two** and **too** in it.

3. Write a sentence that has **they're**, **there** and **their** in it.

4. Write two sentences for each pair of homophones below to show you know the different meanings of the words.

   a) bough/bow

   b) root/route

   c) serial/cereal

   d) grate/great

   e) waist/waste

   f) brake/break

   g) fined/find

   h) bare/bear

Rhyming

Sometimes **rhyming** words contain the **same** letter patterns.
Sometimes **rhyming** words sound alike but have **different** letter patterns.

I **wish** I had a **fish** in a **dish**.

Don't **chew** my best **blue shoe**!

Practice

Copy the lists and match the rhyming words using lines.

1. sway   five
   fly   tall
   drive   tray
   small   see
   tree   cry

2. shine   alarm
   farm   measure
   above   wriggle
   giggle   fine
   treasure   glove

More to think about

1. Copy out and match each word in Set A with its rhyming word in Set B.

Set A

learn	boot	chalk	take	plain
purse	hate	store	boat	sneeze

Set B

squawk	wrote	please	burn	straight
break	verse	raw	cane	suit

2. Copy these words. Underline the odd word in each set.

   a) cart   start   wart   dart

   b) moth   both   cloth   broth

   c) rough   tough   enough   cough

   d) mice   twice   nice   office

   e) post   cost   lost   frost

   f) meat   great   seat   beat

Now try these

The answers to these clues are pairs of rhyming words. Copy the questions and complete the answers with the second rhyming word.

1. a joyful race = fun _____

2. a young hen that is ill = sick _____

3. a fizzy drink store = pop _____

4. a conceited horse rider = cocky _____

5. blonde locks = fair _____

6. recipe collection = cook _____

7. an angry employer = cross _____

Using a dictionary

Dictionaries are arranged in alphabetical order.

To arrange words in **alphabetical order**, you start by looking at the **first** letter in each word. If the **first** letter in each word is the same, you have to look at the **second** letters. If these are the same, you have to look at the **third** letters and so on.

These words are arranged in **alphabetical order** according to the third letter because the first two letters are the same.

co<u>d</u>e   co<u>l</u>d   co<u>r</u>k   co<u>s</u>t

Here they are arranged on a dictionary page.

Dictionaries give us definitions (the meanings of words).

code   a series of letters or symbols used for a secret message

cold   1. at a low temperature
        2. an illness causing sneezing

cork   a stopper for a bottle

cost   an amount given or required as payment

Some words have more than one definition.

Dictionaries help us check spellings.

Practice

1. Answer these questions using the dictionary extract on page 11.

    a) Which word is an illness?

    b) What's a cork?

    c) Which word is used when sending a secret message?

2. Write these words in alphabetical order according to the third letter.

    a) badger, baby, basin, ball

    b) acorn, acrobat, accident, ache

    c) pear, penguin, pebble, peck

More to think about

1. Write the word that comes **after** each of these words in your dictionary.

    a) bulb   b) glitter

    c) portrait   d) rust

    e) crumple   f) famous

    g) metal   h) roof

2. Write the word that comes **before** each of these words in your dictionary.

    a) ripe   b) usual

    c) vandal   d) idle

    e) currant   f) kettle

    g) purr   h) wharf

Now try these

Use the definitions to help you find these words in your dictionary.

1. la _ _ _ _ _ _ _ _ _ _   a room where scientists work

     la _ _   a long string to fasten your shoes

     la _ _ _   a large spoon with a long handle for serving soup

     la _ _ _ _ _ _   words we use when speaking or writing

     la _ _   volcanic rock that is red hot

2. sha _ _   an area of darkness not reached by the sun

     sha _ _ _   with long, thick, untidy hair

     sha _ _ _ _   not deep

     sha _ _ _ _   liquid for washing hair

     sha _ _ _ _   break suddenly into small pieces

Compound words

A word that consists of **two smaller words** joined together is called a **compound word**.

book + mark = bookmark

Sometimes it's **easy** to hear how the word should be spelled when we say it.

cup + board = cupboard

Sometimes it's **hard** to hear how the word should be spelled when we say it.

Practice

Copy these word sums and write the compound words you make.

1. bull + dog = _____

2. butter + fly = _____

3. play + ground = _____

4. egg + cup = _____

5. arm + chair = _____

6. oat + cake = _____

7. table + cloth = _____

8. fire + work = _____

9. sun + light = _____

10. wish + bone = _____

More to think about

Think of a compound word beginning with each of the following words and write them down.

1. foot_____
2. door_____
3. tea_____
4. cross_____
5. back_____
6. butter_____
7. home_____
8. water_____
9. key_____
10. tooth____
11. side_____
12. moon_____

Now try these

1. Copy the lists and use lines to join these words to make compound words.

   post   man
   straw   bag
   tomb   ache
   hedge   stone
   hand   card
   tooth   berry
   gentle   bin
   dust   hog

2. Now underline the tricky bit in each compound word that isn't pronounced.

Common root words

Prefixes and suffixes are added to **root words** to modify their meaning. These words have the same **root word**.

Root word: **phone**

tele**phone**

micro**phone**

Practice

1. Copy the words. Underline the root word in each.

   a) farmer   farming
   b) shopper   shopping
   c) undo   doing
   d) return   turned
   e) kindness   unkind
   f) excited   excitement

2. Write a sentence using each of the root words you've found in 1. For example:

   There are some chickens on the farm.

More to think about

1. Copy these root words. Add two more words that use the same root word.

   a) music   <u>musical</u>   <u>musician</u>

   b) sign

   c) book

   d) plant

   e) high

   f) quick

   g) place

   h) colour

2. Write five sentences, each using one of the words you added.

Now try these

Copy the root words below. Join the prefixes and suffixes in the box to the root words. Make a list of as many words as you can.

ly	un	ful	able	mis	super	inter

love   perfect   wise   sure   fair   correct   take   related

man   national   help   star   behave

Diminutives

Diminutives are words that imply something small.
Sometimes diminutives are made by adding a **prefix**.
Sometimes diminutives are made by adding a **suffix**.

a **mini**-market (a small shop)

an eag**let** (a small eagle)

Practice

Copy these words. Join each with its diminutive form by using a line.

1. eagle   owlet
2. cod   bullock
3. duck   gosling
4. goose   eaglet
5. bull   duckling
6. owl   codling

More to think about

Write the correct definitions for the diminutives.

1. statuette   a small kitchen
2. kitchenette   a small stream
3. mini-series   a small drop of liquid
4. droplet   a small ornamental figure
5. nestling   a short series
6. streamlet   a young bird, still in the nest

Now try these

1. Choose the correct prefix or suffix to complete each diminutive. Use a dictionary to help you if necessary.

let	mini	icle	ette

a) ic_____

b) _____skirt

c) book_____

d) cub_____

e) pig_____

f) pip_____

2. Now write a definition for each word.

Using *its* and *it's*

When do you use **its** or **it's**?

It's with an apostrophe stands for **it is** or **it has**.

Its means **belonging to**.

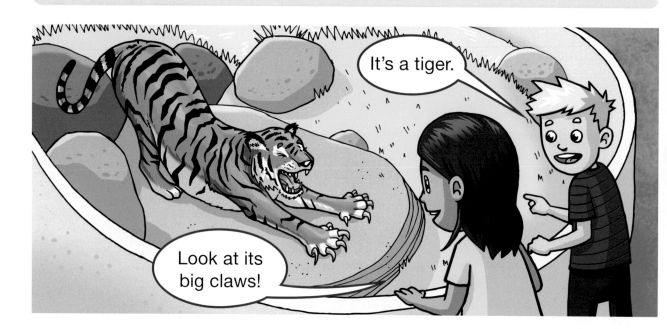

It's a tiger.

Look at its big claws!

Practice

Copy the sentences. Choose *its* or *it's* to fill each gap.

1. "_____ been a very hot day," said Fiona.

2. "_____ the last week of the school holidays tomorrow," James reminded his friends.

3. The rabbit popped out of _____ hole.

4. "_____ got to be the best film I've ever seen," reported Sophie.

5. "_____ time to go out to play," Mrs Carless quietly said.

6. The dog chewed _____ bone.

7. The tree was very big until _____ branch fell off when the snow settled on it.

Copy the passage. Choose *its* or *it's* to fill each gap.

A trip to the beach

"_____ been a terrible day," the family agreed as they drove home in their car. It had all started in the morning when Mum said, "_____ a lovely day and the sun is out. Let's go to the beach."

Once they arrived Dad said, "_____ got to be the busiest I've ever seen!" A dog ran up and shook _____ wet body all over them.

The children ran into the sea, nearly stepping on a crab. It snapped _____ claws. Suddenly dark clouds covered the sky.

"_____ raining," called Mum. "Quick, _____ time to get out of the water."

They jumped in the car soaking wet, but … "Oh, no! _____ not going to start. _____ out of petrol!" they all groaned.

Two hours later they were finally on their way home.

Now try these

1. Write four sentences using its.
2. Write four sentences using it's.

Over-used words

Sometimes we use **the same word too often**.

We can make our writing more accurate or more interesting if we **choose different words or expressions**.

It was a **nice** day so we went for a **nice** walk around the **nice** garden.

It was a **sunny** day so we went for a **short** walk around the **beautiful** garden.

Practice

1. Copy these phrases. Replace the word **good** in each phrase with another word.

   a) a **good** idea   b) a **good** book   c) a **good** time

   d) a **good** holiday   e) a **good** shot   f) a **good** meal

2. Copy the sentences. Replace the word **nice** in each sentence with another word.

   a) The party was very **nice**.

   b) I put on some **nice** clothes.

   c) Our house is very **nice**.

   d) My mum baked some **nice** cakes.

   e) My friend is very **nice**.

   f) It was a **nice** surprise.

More to think about

Rewrite this passage. Leave out the word "then" every time it appears. Which passage sounds better?

I walked into the bookshop and saw an interesting book. **Then** I picked it up and looked at the cover. **Then** I saw it was about magic. **Then** I opened it and looked at the pictures. **Then** I read one of the spells. I began to feel strange. **Then** suddenly my hair started to grow and turn green. **Then** people looked at me and screamed. **Then** I saw myself in a mirror. I had turned into a monster!

Now try these

1. Use a thesaurus to find some synonyms for these words:

   a) nice   b) good   c) got

2. Copy the passage and substitute your own words for the words in bold.

We have a **nice** dog called Smudge. Last Sunday we had a **nice** day in the countryside. Smudge had a **good** time rolling in all the mud. When we **got** home we decided to give Smudge a **good** bath. We **got** her in the bath and tried to give her a **good** wash. Smudge **got** rather cross. She **got** out of the bath and ran into the kitchen. She gave herself a **good** shake all over the **nice** clean floor. Then she **got** out of the back door. When we **got** her back we **got** her dry with some old towels. Smudge smells very **nice** again now. What a **good** dog she is!

Gender

The gender of a person or an animal is either **masculine** (male) or **feminine** (female).

The word **queen** is **feminine**. The word **king** is **masculine**.

The queen waved to the crowds.
The king sat and smiled.

Practice

Copy these sets of words. Join the two words that make a pair with a line.

1. feminine	masculine	2. feminine	masculine
mother	brother	cow	tiger
sister	nephew	lioness	bull
daughter	uncle	hen	lion
aunt	father	tigress	drake
niece	son	duck	cockerel

More to think about

1. Copy the words and add the suffix *ess*
   to these masculine words to make them feminine.
   Write the word.

   a) baron   b) count

   c) host   d) heir

   e) lion   f) giant

2. Copy these words. Beside each word, write (m) if it's masculine
   or (f) if it's feminine. Use a dictionary if necessary.

   a) grandmother   b) duchess

   c) bridegroom   d) goddess

   e) monk   f) lord

   g) mare   h) ewe

   i) vixen   j) widow

   k) gander   l) prince

3. Now write the opposite of each of the words above.

Now try these

**Copy these sentences. Change the words in bold into
the opposite gender.**

1. The **princess** rode a horse.

2. The **cow** was grazing in the meadow.

3. The **landlord** of the hotel was very helpful.

4. The **fox** was in the woods.

5. The **duchess** put on **her** best clothes.

6. The **bride** arrived early. **She** came by car.

7. The **lion** roared loudly in the bush.

8. Hissing angrily, the **goose** flapped at the gate.

Our living language

Our **language** changes all the time.

Words die out and new words come in.

The way we say things changes over a period of time.

I'm going to listen to the wireless.

I'm going to listen to the radio.

Thou art a beauteous damsel.

You're a beautiful woman.

Practice

Copy this list of words. Underline the words that you think have entered our language only in the past 150 years.

a) astronaut
b) supermarket
c) cart
d) light

e) computer
f) glass
g) farm
h) internet

i) rain
j) refrigerator
k) radio
l) pencil

More to think about

1. Copy the old words in Set A in a list down your page. Next to each word, write the word in Set B that means the same. Use a dictionary to help you.

Set A

| frock | omnibus | perambulator | butt | quaff |
| kin | spectacles | bonnet | satchel | pitcher |

Set B

| glasses | pram | drink | dress | bus |
| barrel | schoolbag | relatives | hat | jug |

2. Write these words. Match each word with its definition. Use a dictionary if necessary.

a) cobbler   a measure of liquid

b) guinea   a sitting-room

c) quart   an old English coin

d) scuttle   a cup for drinking out of

e) parlour   someone who mends shoes

f) tinker   food

g) goblet   a container for coal

h) victuals   someone who mends pots and pans

Now try these

Try writing this conversation in modern English!

Sire. Pray allow thy humble servant to replenish thy goblet.

Behold, thou careless varlet! My goblet runneth over onto my doublet. Get thee gone afore thou dost commit any more mischief.

Standard and non-standard English

Standard English is the form of English that's recognised and most widely used.

Non-standard English can be when different regions use their own words or phrases (dialect/slang) or when the grammar in Standard English speech or text is incorrect.

Standard English — I don't want any help.

Non-standard English — I don't want no help.

Practice

All these words are slang words from Australia and Liverpool. Copy the words and write them with their correct meanings.

Australian slang	Meaning	Liverpudlian slang	Meaning
chook	friend	yis	breakfast
cozzie	no problem	brekky	I say
postie	chicken	scran	Is that so?
mate	present	ta	yes
no worries	swimming costume	darrafact?	food or snack
prezzy	postman/woman	ay ay	thanks

No worries

Ay, ay

More to think about

Look at these sentences carefully.
Write each of them in Standard English.

1. I ain't never done nothin' like that.

2. She jumped off of the wall into the pool.

3. Yousef can do that quicklier than you.

4. You'ze lot've got to come home for tea.

5. There's the tap we drinked from.

6. If he hadn't've stayed in bed he wouldn't of been late.

Now try these

1. Some people use a **rhyming slang**. This rhyming slang is from London and is called Cockney rhyming slang. Use the Cockney rhyming slang in your own sentences.

   a) lump of lead = head

   b) apples and pears = stairs

   c) frog and toad = road

   d) mince pies = eyes

   e) Barnet Fair = hair

2. Make up your own rhyming slang for these words.

   a) bag

   b) book

   c) school

   d) tea

Progress Unit

1. Copy these words. Write the correct definition with each word.

cabin	not heavy, easy to lift
hospital	soft shoes worn indoors
light	a building where ill people are cared for
saddle	a small room on a ship
slippers	a seat on a horse

2. Copy these rhyming words. Write another word to go with each pair.

a) stair, wear

b) date, great

c) coat, note

d) come, thumb

e) here, steer

f) learn, turn

3. Write the correct word for each picture.

hair   hare   ball   bawl   break   brake   pale   pail

4. Write a word that would come between these words in a dictionary.

a) **pancake** and **parcel**

b) **envelope** and **ewe**

c) **stick** and **stupid**

5. Copy these words. Join them to make compound words.

book	brush
pen	cake
tooth	knife
fire	bag
pan	board
tea	shoe
horse	case
card	work

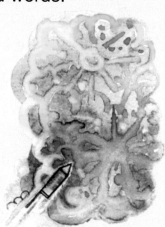

6. Write the words in Set A in a list down your page. Then write each word from Set B that has the same root word alongside. Underline the root word like this: dis<u>comfort</u>, <u>comfort</u>er

Set A
shopper   unfriendly
powerful   action
cleanest   misunderstand

Set B
friendliness   cleanly
actor   understandable
empower   shopping

7. Copy and complete each sentence.
A duckling is a small _____.
An owlet is a small _____.
An eaglet is a small _____.
A gosling is a small _____.

8. Copy the sentences. Choose *it's* or *its* to complete each one.

a) The baby played with _____ rattle.

b) _____ a lovely day today.

c) My dog has lost _____ lead.

d) I know _____ here somewhere!

e) Can't you see that _____ been ripped?

f) The fire engine raced down the street with _____ siren going.

9. Rewrite each sentence. Change the word in bold for a better word.

a) I **got** home late.

b) She **got** very angry.

c) Sunday was a **nice** day.

d) I had a **nice** lunch.

e) The cake was **good**.

f) I had a **good** sleep.

10. Copy these nouns. Write whether each one is masculine (m) or feminine (f).

a) princess   b) husband

c) bride   d) niece

e) brother   f) uncle

g) wife   h) son

11. Copy the table. Write each word in the box in the correct column.

Newer words	Older words
helicopter	farthing

helicopter farthing computer hark video robot
monocle cinders television radar breeches bonnet

12. Write these sentences in Standard English.

a) Ain't we goin' to the shoe shop?

b) I've finded the missing puzzle piece.

c) Lucy's prezzy was the beautifulest china doll.